Live This Life

Live This Life

10 Top Tips for Living a Happier Life & Why Positive Thinking Works

Mark Dawes

Author of Understanding Quantum Thinking

"The highest art is the art
of living an ordinary life in
an extraordinary manner."

Tibetan Proverb

Live This Life
By Mark Dawes

Published in 2012 by NFPS Ltd.

Hampshire, England.
www.nfps.info

Printed by Bell and Bain Ltd,. Glasgow

TABLE OF CONTENTS

INTRODUCTION

I have written this book for those of you who maybe experiencing current personal problems in your life, and for those of you who maybe experiencing change in your life and the uncertainty that change brings. I have also written this book for those of you who maybe experiencing pain in your life, be it either physical or mental, and for those of you are exposed to the unhealthy and unkind words and acts of others whose aim may be to destroy you or demoralise you into giving up and failing. I have also written this book for those of you who feel 'stuck' in a set of circumstances or in an environment in which you just feel like giving up because you cannot see any light at the end of the tunnel. This book is also intended for those of you who are unsure of where your life is taking you at this present moment in time and possibly do not know what path to follow.

My aim in writing this book is to give you a few key tools and concepts and a definitive strategy to help you change your life for the better, despite how you may be feeling and in-spite of your current emotional state and circumstances.

However I cannot take any accolades for what I'm about to write as none of this has anything to do with me. What I'm about to share with you is information that has found its way to me at some stage of my life. In essence, everything I'm about to tell you is universally available to everyone and anyone, and therefore no credit can be given to me at all. All I see myself in this process is someone who can signpost you along a route that will help you make better decisions, that I guarantee will improve the quality of your life for the better, should you choose to follow the advice in this book.

This book is fundamentally all about your mental attitude and how you choose to approach your life. Therefore, the mental attitude in which you read this book will also determine the meaning found within the information you uncover, and the purpose that meaning can provide for you in your life.

Your mental attitude is really important. It is the major factor, which attracts people to you in the spirit of friendliness, or repels them, according to whether your attitude is positive or negative; and you're the only person who can determine which it shall be.

If you are a businessperson or salesperson then your mental attitude, regardless of what you are selling, will determine your success or failure, irrespective of market conditions or the state of the economy.

Your mental attitude also determines, to a large extent, whether you find peace of mind or go through life in a state of frustration and misery.

In essence your mental attitude controls, very largely, the space you occupy in your life, the success you achieve, the friends you make and the contribution you make to future generations. In short, it will be no great overstatement of the truth if we were to state that mental attitude is everything.

Your mental attitude is the last bastion of control. It is the one and only thing over which anyone has been given a complete, unchallengeable privilege of personal control. The real unequivocal truth is that the only person who can dictate or choose their mental attitude at any given time and in any given set of circumstances is you. Others cannot take it from you, you have to give it away or hand over control. Once you understand this you are on your way to discovering one of the greatest secrets of universal power that every great person, survivor, inventor, explorer, prophet and sage has known throughout time.

It is a false truth however, to believe that we can control the thoughts and actions of other people. Trying to do so in an effort to lessen the negative effect of their thoughts, actions and deeds, only serves to increase our own frustration, anxiety, our fears and our distress.

The skill in mastering your mind is also relatively simple, but to do so you will need to do three things as preparation for this task if you are serious about achieving mastery of your life and living your life to its full potential. The first is to have a clear defined purpose of what you want to achieve and then suspend all disbelief, nagging doubts and internal criticism. What I mean by this is, not to give up before you even try because you can't imagine or see an immediate benefit straight away. Now, this does not mean that you have to have your life's ultimate goal clearly defined already, or have a five-year plan in place for the achievement of a major goal. It simply means having a clear understanding of the things you want in your life, be they short term or long term goals, that will move you forward as opposed to holding you back. For those of you who are going to be relatively new to this kind of thinking may I suggest that to start with, you set yourself some smaller achievable goals that will motivate you to take action, so that you can see the benefit of what you are about to prove to yourself relatively quickly and easily.

Secondly, never give up. At the beginning you may find some things difficult, but you should never give up, because continual effort, no matter how small, in a defined direction can create massive changes over time, as you will soon realise as you read through this book.

Thirdly, do not accept failure nor see any setback as a form of failure. Keep on going no matter what. Use everything as feedback, making minor adjustments where necessary to move you towards your clearly defined purpose.

Just think about this. If you could make one small change a day that would change your life within two months would you be willing to try? If the answer to that question is no then simply put this book down now. However, if you are willing to explore that possibility and suspend any negative belief, nagging doubt or the small voice of internal criticism, then read on.

CHAPTER 1
50 Folds of Paper

What you are about to read now is taken from book called "The Tipping Point" by Malcolm Gladwell.

"Consider, for example, the following puzzle. I give you a large piece of paper, and I ask you to fold it over once, and then take that fold of paper and fold it over again, and then again, and again, until you have refolded the original paper 50 times. How tall do think the final stack is going to be? In answer to that question, most people will fold the sheet in their minds eye, and guess that the pile would be as thick as a phone book or, if really courageous, they'll say it would be as tall as a refrigerator. But the real answer is that the height of the stack would approximate the distance to the sun. And if you folded it over one more time, the stack would be as high as the distance to the sun and back. This is an example of what in mathematics is called a geometric progression. Epidemics are another example of geometric progression: when a virus spreads through a population, it doubles and doubles again, until it has (figuratively) grown from a single sheet of paper all the way to the sun in 50 steps. As human beings we have a hard time with this kind of progression, because the end result – the effect – seems far out of proportion to the cause. To appreciate the power of epidemics, we have to abandon this expectation about proportionality. We need to prepare ourselves for the possibility that sometimes big changes follow from small events, and that sometimes these changes can happen very quickly."

This is why, one of the first things you need to do in order to create massive change in your life, is to suspend any limiting disbeliefs.

There also seems to be something special with regards to the number 50. When you were first conceived, for example, you were a single strand of double DNA in your mother's ovum. That one, single strand, divided 50 times only and in 50 replications it became 100 trillion cells (which is more than all the stars in the Milky Way Galaxy), with each cell doing a phenomenal 6 trillion things a second. Don't believe me? Then watch the following You Tube video and be amazed:

http://www.youtube.com/watch?v=-4GtimvTX6Q

Now think about this. How many times does an infant child fall over before it finally takes its first step unaided? It is certainly more than 50. In fact it is probably hundreds of attempts if not thousands. And the child will keep on falling over because it simply applies 3 simple rules:

1. It has a clear defined purpose of what it wants to achieve – it wants to walk,

2. It will never give up until it finally achieves its desired objective, which is to walk unaided, and

3. It has no concept of failing because it doesn't know what failure is (it hasn't been taught that as yet). The child simply makes minor adjustments and improvements' to each effort it takes in moving towards its clearly defined purpose.

I guarantee you that if you apply these 3 simple rules to your life from now on, you can only move forward and improve your life for the better.

What I would like you to understand from the information in this chapter is that you, as a human being, are capable of geometric progression. You must be, because that is how you developed from one single strand of DNA. Therefore, if you apply the same 'epidemic' to your thinking, can you now see what you are really capable of? And you have the God given capability to do so and all of the universal resources available to you to make it happen.

CHAPTER 2
You Are God-Like

It is a well-established fact in all the major religions of the world that God gave everyone free will. The only reason the Creator did so was to give you complete control over your thinking. Why? - To allow us to be Creators too, to be the designers of our destiny and the architects of how we choose to live our life and that proof exists in the Bible.

In the Gospels of the New Testament Jesus said that the kingdom of heaven exists in each and everyone of us, and that God made us all in his image. If this were true, why then would God, who created you in his image, produce a flawed copy? The fact is he didn't. You are perfect in every way and all the power, resources and energy of the universe is universally available to you as it is to God himself – and you have to work very hard to screw that up!

In the Gospel of Thomas, one of the Gnostic Gospels that was found in a cave in Nag Hammadi, the Disciple Thomas states that Jesus said: *"If those who lead you say to you, 'See, the kingdom [of heaven] is in the sky,' then the birds of the sky will precede you. If they say to you, 'It is in the sea,' then the fish will precede you. Rather, the kingdom [of heaven] is inside of you, and it is outside of you. When you come to know yourselves, then you will become known, and you will realize that it is you who are the sons of the living father. But if you will not know yourselves, you dwell in poverty, and it is you who are that poverty."*

What this means is that heaven, and all of its wonder, isn't to be found anywhere outside of you. It exists inside of you, but to access it you need to know yourself and realise that you are God-like. You are the creator of your world.

Also in that extract from the Gospel of Thomas the word *"poverty"* is used, but it is used in context to describe a person's thinking, not their financial or social status. What it translates to is: think in terms of poverty and you will live in poverty because you will never recognise the universal power and resources available to you that you already possess. However, think in terms of abundance and you live in abundance. The Gospels also say that Jesus said: *"Ask and it shall be given to you. Knock and doors shall be opened to you"*. What the Gospels don't tell you to do though, is ask intelligently and to make sure that you knock at the right door!

A positive mental attitude therefore, is the habit of keeping the mind busily engaged in connection with the circumstance of things one desires in life, and away from things one does not desire. However, the vast majority of people will go all the way through their life with a mental attitude attuned to what they do not want. Their mental attitudes are dominated by fears and anxieties and worries over circumstances, which somehow have a way of making appearances later. In short, they create that which they fear the most. They ask for the wrong things and knock on the wrong doors.

To emphasise this point more clearly consider this. Sometimes when you go shopping you will make a shopping list, and on that list you will write all of the things that you must remember to buy, because you either need them or want them. Have you ever considered writing a shopping list of all of the things that you definitely do not want and that you must remember not to buy because you definitely do not need them? Well the answer to that should be a resounding no, because there would simply be no point, and if you did you would probably end up coming back from the shops without some of the items you wanted or needed because you were too busy thinking about what you didn't want.

Yet when it comes to our lives, how many people can give you 'lists' of things that they definitely do not want, but when asked what they do want they draw a blank? Then, when what they do not want materialises they say: *"why does it always happen to me?"*

Well the reason is if you keep on focussing on what you don't want in life you'll eventually get what you don't want because you'll help create the situations and circumstances that will give rise to the possibility of it materialising. The Chinese even have a proverb for that which says: *"Be careful what you wish for"*.

The worst part of this tragedy is that these people who do this actually blame other people for the misfortunes that they have brought upon themselves by their own negative mental attitude. Yet blame is only an excuse for lack of personal responsibility.

However, someone who is trained in how to use their mind will find the seed of an equivalent benefit in every set of circumstances presented to them. In short, they find meaning and purpose in everything, good or bad, and have developed a natural ability to turn any adversity into their advantage.

More importantly, they take responsibility for their lives and refuse to live in someone else's limited mind-set and dogma.

CHAPTER 3
Let's go down the mind gym

An example of someone who has this ability is an elite athlete. Elite athletes learn how to block out images representing doubt, which is an important skill if you wish to become successful and perform at the highest level.

What they become experts at is when an image of difficulty or negativity pops into their heads, they become extremely adept at changing the internal movie, quickly editing it to imagine success. This skill is as important - if not more important - than any physical training they do. They look to the future with definiteness of purpose and focus on it so it becomes a permanent fixture in their minds eye, like a lighthouse that stops negativity dashing their hopes and aspirations on the rocks of failure.

Tip 1: Be definite in your positive outlook to life. Set your sights on what you want, as opposed to what you don't want, and you can start by changing all negative thoughts to positive ones. Engage all of your senses in doing this, just as you did when you were a child.

Experienced athletes engage all of their senses in their mental rehearsal. They do not only have a visual, internal image of the future event, they also hear it, feel it, smell it and taste it. They are fully focused on the outcome they desire and not on failure. This does not mean however, that at times they do not fail. In fact athletes fail 85% to 95% of the time. However, they do not see this as failure, they find the seed of equivalent benefit in the output that they have produced, and look for ways of incorporating learning and meaning as a means of constructive feedback to improve their performance, thus aiding them in moving closer towards the ultimate goal or outcome they desire.

Why do they do this? They understand the relationship between the mind and the body. They understand that the electrical activity produced by the brain is identical, whether they are thinking about doing something or actually doing it, and this is because the brain does not distinguish between perception and reality (actually doing something or simply thinking about doing something). Either way, the neural networks associated with what they are doing or thinking about doing, grow directly in proportion to how much they do it or think about it. In essence the mental rehearsal that they use lays down the tracks to success just as well as physical practice does.

Now, here's how to do it.

Think about what it is you would like to achieve and create a clear mental picture of what it is in your mind's eye. It may be that you wish to see yourself as being happier or more relaxed, or it may be seeing yourself as being successful in your chosen field. Whatever it is, focus your mind on what your defined outcome is intended to be and create a clear mental picture of it, as though it has already been achieved.

Now find somewhere quiet. Sit back in a comfortable chair and relax. Place your hands on your abdomen – right hand over left and uncross your legs. Close your eyes to remove all outside influences and simply focus on your breath. Notice how when you breathe in you feel your abdomen rise, and when you breathe out you notice your abdomen deflate. That is why your hands are there.

Breathe normally. Do not make it a contrived effort. Just gently breathe in and out paying full attention to the rhythm and flow of your breath, whilst noticing the rise and the fall of your abdomen. If at any stage whilst doing this a distracting thought enters your mind, let it in, then let it out and bring your attention back to your breath. The object of the exercise is to open your mind up, not create a fortress mentality.

Do this for approximately five minutes until you are comfortable with the rhythm and flow of your breath.

Now focus your mind on your objective – your desired outcome. Bring back the picture you created at the beginning, of yourself in your desired state, as though it has already been achieved. Don't try too hard, just let it appear and manifest itself in your minds eye. At first this may seem difficult. If it does do not try harder, simply bring your attention back to your breathing and just trust that your desired outcome will appear when ready.

When it does, focus on only the positive aspects of what you can see. Notice how much more happier you are or how much more relaxed you are, in your mind's image or notice how much more successful you have just become. Whatever your defined outcome is, create it as clearly as you can.

Now, because this is all happening in your mind, we can use your mind's universal power to do whatever we like with it to enhance the experience. So, make the image you have created clearer and crisper. Make the colours brighter and bolder. Increase the size and notice how the intensity of what you are experiencing is being enhanced.

If you can hear any sounds, such as music or positive dialogue, make them clearer and louder.

If you have any good feelings in your body associated with what you are now seeing and hearing, intensify those feelings so that they feel really good – remember, because this is all happening in your mind you can do whatever you like because you are working with one of the greatest virtual reality machines in the universe.

Now, there will be two perspectives that you will be viewing this from. You will either be experiencing this as though you are looking through your own eyes, or you will be seeing yourself in the image as if looking through someone else's eyes. If it is the latter I want you now to do this. Simply see yourself in the desired future state that you have created, and then see yourself stepping into the "you" that you have become in the future, and notice any differences in how that may make you feel as you do it.

Do this for approximately five minutes to start (you can lengthen the time with each practice if you like). Then, once you feel that you have done it long enough simply bring your attention back to your breathing for a few minutes, whilst basking in the new positive image that you have created and the new positive feelings that you have generated in you. Then, when you are ready, simply give yourself the intention of opening your eyes only as slowly or as fast as you would like to do so.

Once fully awake take a while to reflect on what you have just achieved, which is actually a phenomenal feat, and any positive changes that you notice in yourself. You may be pleasantly surprised.

I cannot emphasise to you enough the importance of this one technique. It is used by many successful people the world over and is one of the stable techniques in NLP (Neuro-Linguistic Programming). Yet it is not a new technique. Buddhist monks have been using it for thousands of years to achieve 'bodhichitta', which means 'enlightened mind'. Now Buddhists are the 'Olympic Athletes' of meditation, so if it's good enough for them, it's good enough for me!

By doing this you have started programming your mind and setting your unconscious 'servo-mechanism' on the right course towards the right target.

CHAPTER 4
Your Unconscious 'Servo-Mechanism' to Success

In Maxwell Maltz's book Psycho-Cybernetics, he refers to the subconscious mind not as a mind but as "servo-mechanism". He states that the creative mechanism within all individuals is impersonal and is designed to help us achieve goals of success and happiness, or unhappiness and distress, depending upon how this "servo-mechanism" is programmed.

Like any other servo-mechanism, it must have clear-cut goal, objective, or "problem" to work upon. Once programmed this goal striving mechanism acts like a guidance system within a torpedo designed to automatically steer it in the direction required to hit the target that it has been programmed to seek.

And, just like any other servo-mechanism, it will work directly upon information and data that we feed into it by our attitudes, thoughts, beliefs, interpretations or perceptions. Because when we do that we "describe" the target to be hit or the problem to be worked upon.

Feed information and data into a creative servo-mechanism, to the effect that we are unworthy, inferior, undeserving, incapable, etc., and this data will be processed and acted upon to guide us to a target that will support those negatively held and limiting beliefs.

However, if we choose to consciously input data and information into our unconscious mind that we are; worthy, capable, intelligent, deserving, etc., then our inbuilt guidance system will automatically program itself to find a target deserving of the data we have programmed and keep us on course towards our desired outcome.

In short we will look for the opportunity or disappointment necessary to ensure that the 'missile' reaches its target.

The key therefore, lies in what information and data the programmer chooses to input. That is where you come in. You need to choose what information you wish to input. You are the 'programmer' of your unconscious 'servo-mechanism'.

Tip 2: Consciously and continually make every effort to only program information and data via the tools of autosuggestion and self-talk that are both positive and beneficial. In addition, keep practicing the exercise at the end of the previous chapter as regularly and as often as you can.

CHAPTER 5
The Mind as a Fertile Field

Think of your unconscious mind as a fertile field of unending possibility, that will grow any seed you choose to plant, but bear in mind that your unconscious mind, albeit a phenomenal piece of equipment, is also like an obedient servant that will obey whatever command you choose to give it. In short, it will grow whatever seeds you choose to plant.

As a result, if you plant wheat seeds you will gain a crop of wheat, barley seeds a crop of barley, and so on. However, choose to plant weed seeds and you will end up with a crop of weeds.

Now think of your conscious mind as the gatekeeper to the fertile field, the person who decides what seeds get planted and what do not. If your conscious mind is aware and alert it will only allow seeds of a positive value to be planted, such as wheat or barley, and will stop or prevent weed seeds from entering the field, thus preventing any weeds from being grown.

To do this however, your conscious mind has to be trained to notice what is of benefit and what is not, then after a while it will perform it's duties like a well-schooled and experienced sentry.

Therefore, the first thing to do is to become aware of how many negative influences are effecting your thinking and, like a diligent gatekeeper, prevent them access into the field, thus preventing them from having access to the fertile soil that can make them flourish and grow into deep-rooted influences in your life.

Then, train yourself to notice more positive influences in your life and allow them access to the fertile field so that they can benefit from the nutrients that will allow them to grow into more permanent aspects of your identity.

One way you can do this right now is to read and watch only those books and programmes that are going to be of benefit to you and to stop reading and watching anything that can have a detrimental effect on your thinking. By doing this you are controlling access to that fertile field of unending possibilities.

Tip 3: Make a conscious decision, not to read or watch anything that will leave a negative impression in your mind, like muddy footprints on your carpet. Just as you would ask someone to remove their dirty or muddy shoes before entering your home, instruct yourself to restrict entry to the 'home' of your intellect by leaving anything that can 'muddy' your thoughts outside of the entry to the house of your mind.

CHAPTER 6
How to use Autosuggestion and Self-Talk

I have been involved with learning and teaching Neuro–Linguistic Programming for many years now and I just want to explain to you for a moment my take on what one aspect of what Neuro–Linguistic Programming means to me.

Neuro, as you are probably aware, means neurological or how we use our brain and mind. Linguistic obviously means language, and programming is how your language (internal and external dialogue) influences and programmes your neurology.

As human beings we use between 45,000 - 60,000 words a day in the form of internal dialogue, and in addition they also have between 60,000 - 80,000 thoughts a day. Now most people are not aware that they use such a large amount of internal dialogue or have so many thoughts, because all of this is happening at an unconscious level below what we are consciously aware of. However, it does have an effect on our outlook in life because it is constantly programming that unconscious 'servo-mechanism' and defining its target. It is also responsible for the 'seed-thoughts' that are planted in your unconscious mind, which is why it is so important to understand this concept fully.

Imagine for a moment that I arrive at your front door 45,000 - 60,000 times a day and each time you open the door to me I say: *"your useless, your worthless, you will never amount to anything, it's always your fault"*. After a very short period of time my ability to expose you to such high degrees of negativity will have a most definite effect on what you end up thinking about and also your own internal dialogue (what you say to yourself), which will ultimately result in what you will choose to focus on.

In addition, if my input creates the ability for you to relive what I have said by repeating it over and over again to yourself, you (like an elite athlete) are practising mental rehearsal and in doing so are now choosing to program (like a series of coded software instructions to control the operation of a computer) your own mind without any further help from me.

To overcome this you simply need to replace the negative and critical self-talk with a more positive narrative and dialogue. Say nice things to yourself, complement yourself and others, and re-affirm your beauty, ability and capacity for positive growth. It is important that you do this regularly and continually, due to the vast amount of negativity that we are exposed to on a consistent basis throughout the day from various sources such as the television, radio, newspapers and other people – including close friends and family.

As Muhammad Ali said: *"I am the greatest. I said that even before I knew I was"*. He also went onto say: *"It is the repetition of affirmations that lead to belief. And once that belief becomes a deep conviction, things begin to happen"*.

Tip 4: Replace negative criticism with positive self-talk at every opportunity.

To do this, it is vitally important that you:

a) Identify, recognise and stop any unhealthy and unnecessary internal negative criticism, and

b) Replace it with positive, healthy and constructive internal self-talk.

Do this regularly and consistently and I guarantee that this will change your life.

CHAPTER 7
What Doesn't Kill us Makes us Stronger

From my experience I have discovered that the Creator never singled out any individual for important service to mankind without first testing him or her through struggle in proportion to the nature of the services to render. Why? - Because through struggle we become stronger.

Currently in today's society, here in the UK, many people live with the fear of uncertainty. They are worried about their jobs, their future, their financial situation and their health, and all this can have a negative impact on their perception of the future and on their current relationships. However it is possible that there is a reason for us as a human race to need to experience such setbacks, as part of our need for full psychological, spiritual, emotional and even physical growth. It also now seems that science is beginning to understand and recognise the process and the benefits of these setbacks to us as human beings, and this is something that a great woman called Angela Patmore has uncovered in her book 'Challenging Depression and Despair'.

In Angela's book she informs us that in recent years, Nobel Prize-winning scientists like Murray Gell-Mann, Philip Anderson and Kenneth Arrow, have been studying what science refers to as 'complex systems'. Examples of complex systems are: piles of sand, pans of simmering water, the money markets, artificial intelligence, insect swarms, bird flocks, tornados, storm clouds, etc. What they have found is that all of these systems exhibit a strange transition that scientists have named 'emergence' and one of the complex systems under study is the human brain.

What 'emergence' means is that at the highest point of tension, and on the very edge of chaos, they 'change gear' and spontaneously produce order.

For example, a pan of water is put on to boil. All the little water molecules behave more and more randomly and chaotically until suddenly, as though at the throwing of a switch, they all organise into a hexagonal convection pattern and simmer. From the very edge of chaos emerges order.

But what does this mean to us?

What it means is that experiencing fear, distress and uncertainty and being exposed to tension and conflict may be absolutely crucial and vital to our brain's ability to make connections. The actual processes that uncertainty, fear and distress cause us may actually be part of a complex process designed to produce a heightened state of achievement - a gateway to achieving our full potential. This would most certainly explain why creative people go through an emotional loop to produce their best work and why so many people need to work under pressure in order to create the results they really desire.

Without the complex physiological changes that take place in the brain, the brain would not be able to move into its higher gears, create new pathways and break through the neurological limitations that may be preventing excellence from manifesting its true self.

Many great people have achieved great things in situations of personal crisis. Think about the Apollo 13 Space Flight that nearly ended in disaster and how the ground crew and flight-crew managed to find a solution to what seemed an unsolvable problem. Timothy Gallwey, who wrote the "Inner Game, had what can only be referred to as a 'revelation' or an 'epiphany' when he nearly died. Ernest Shackleton the great explorer achieved great feats of endurance to ensure that he brought all of his men home from the doomed exploration to the South Pole, and even great sages and prophets have only found their true vocation after a period of intense crisis. Even Winston Churchill suffered terrible bouts of apathy and despair, but he continually fought them and that strength enabled him to become one of the greatest wartime leaders the world has ever seen, whose speeches galvanized a whole nation into cohesive action.

In short, human beings do not achieve greatness by accepting crisis situations as things beyond our control that we can do nothing about and then simply rolling over and accepting less than what we are worth or capable of. Human beings achieve greatness through crisis, and it would seem from the research and evidence, that we are designed to do so. In fact, how do you think we came to dominate the planet in the first place? Through running away and feeling sorry for ourselves? No. We did it by overcoming adversity by facing it head on and doing something about it. When we do that we 'emerge' victorious and create order from confusion.

It is also no coincidence that a diamond, one of the most beautiful and precious gems on our planet, has to go through years of pressure, hidden in the darkness of the earth before it is finally mined and polished into a beautiful gemstone that is strong enough and tough enough to cut through almost any other material on the planet. Without such pressure and solitude however, it would have never had the capacity to manifest itself into such beauty and reveal its true strength. I believe that we all have the potential to be 'diamonds' given the right circumstances.

As a human race we have known this for millennia and it is why fables and stories such as Beauty and the Beast and the Ugly Ducking exist. True beauty and strength cannot exist without pressure, stress and solitude. These factors are necessary for the transformation of someone into something greater than what they could otherwise be.

But, as we all have free will and free choice we have two options, which are:

1. We can accept confusion, uncertainty and crisis' as being something we can do nothing about and live our lives under a cloud of constant fear and worry, or;

2. We can embrace change, uncertainty and crisis and move forward simply knowing that if we keep on going - sometimes until we reach boiling point – that we will eventually unlock the universal creativity and unlimited potential that resides in all of us.

The real difference, between those who succeed and those who do not, seems to lie in the unequivocal fact that those who can find the seed of equivalent benefit in any drawback or setback are the ones more likely to find meaning in their experience and use it to move them towards the desired goal.

And this is why a positive mental attitude is so very important.

It is absolutely crucial in times of setbacks as a tool for allowing us to look upon all unpleasant circumstances as an opportunity to test one's capacity to rise above such circumstances, by searching for that seed of equivalent benefit and putting it to work.

It also allows us to develop an attitude to make allowances for the frailties and weaknesses of other people, without becoming shocked by the negative mindedness, or influenced by their limited way of thinking.

It also gives us the ability to look for the good qualities in other people, whilst at the same time being prepared to recognise unfavourable qualities in others without being influenced into a negative state of mind by them.

Our mental attitude however, is a two-way gate across the pathway of life, which can be swung one way in success and the other way into failure. The tragedy is that most people swing the gate in the wrong direction. However, take control of how you choose to use your mind and you become the master of your destiny, the captain of your ship.

Tip 5: Consciously make the effort to find the benefit in everything you do. Decide to now ignore any negativity or doubt. Yet should negativity occur consciously rise above it and direct your mind back to finding the positive seed of equivalent benefit in any given situation.

One person of my generation who had an innate capacity to do just that was Steve Jobs, the co-founder and former CEO of Apple Computer who died in 2011. However, in 2005 he gave a speech to the graduating class of Stamford University about his journey through life, which, in my opinion, is one of the most inspiring and motivational speeches I have ever heard.

CHAPTER 8
Joining the Dots of Life – Steve Jobs' Speech

I have included the speech in its entirety here as I believe that it will be an invaluable source of inspiration to all of you who may not know what the future may bring, who fear uncertainty and who are afraid of taking a risk. Enjoy.

For those of you who would rather see and hear the speech you can do so by clicking on the following link:

http://www.youtube.com/watch?v=D1R-jKKp3NA

"I am honoured to be with you today at your commencement from one of the finest universities in the world. I never graduated from college. Truth be told, this is the closest I've ever gotten to a college graduation. Today I want to tell you three stories from my life. That's it. No big deal. Just three stories.

The first story is about connecting the dots.

I dropped out of Reed College [Portland, Oregon] after the first six months, but then stayed around as a drop-in for another 18 months or so before I really quit. So why did I drop out?

It started before I was born. My biological mother was a young, unwed college graduate student, and she decided to put me up for adoption. She felt very strongly that I should be adopted by college graduates, so everything was all set for me to be adopted at birth by a lawyer and his wife. Except that when I popped out they decided at the last minute that they really wanted a girl. So my parents, who were on a waiting list, got a call in the middle of the night asking: "We have an unexpected baby boy; do you want him?" They said: "Of course." My biological mother later found out that my mother had never graduated from college and that my father had never graduated from high school. She refused to sign the final adoption papers. She only relented a few months later when my parents promised that I would someday go to college.

And 17 years later I did go to college. But I naively chose a college that was almost as expensive as Stanford, and all of my working-class parents' savings were being spent on my college tuition. After six months I couldn't see the value in it. I had no idea what I wanted to do with my life and no idea how college was going to help me figure it out. And here I was spending all of the money my parents had saved their entire life. So I decided to drop out and trust that it would all work out OK. It was pretty scary at the time, but looking back it was one of the best decisions I ever made. The minute I dropped out I could stop taking the required classes that didn't interest me, and begin dropping in on the ones that looked interesting.

It wasn't all romantic. I didn't have a dorm room, so I slept on the floor in friends' rooms, I returned Coke bottles for the 5¢ deposits to buy food with, and I would walk the seven miles across town every Sunday night to get one good meal a week at the Hare Krishna temple. I loved it. And much of what I stumbled into by following my curiosity and intuition turned out to be priceless later on. Let me give you one example:

Reed College at that time offered perhaps the best calligraphy instruction in the country. Throughout the campus every poster, every label on every drawer, was beautifully hand calligraphed. Because I had dropped out and didn't have to take the normal classes, I decided to take a calligraphy class to learn how to do this. I learned about serif and sans serif typefaces, about varying the amount of space between different letter combinations, about what makes great typography great. It was beautiful, historical, artistically subtle in a way that science can't capture, and I found it fascinating.

None of this had even a hope of any practical application in my life. But 10 years later, when we were designing the first Macintosh computer, it all came back to me. And we designed it all into the Mac. It was the first computer with beautiful typography. If I had never dropped in on that single course in college, the Mac would have never had multiple typefaces or proportionally spaced fonts. And since Windows just copied the Mac, it's likely that no personal computer would have them. If I had never dropped out, I would have never dropped in on this calligraphy class, and personal computers might not have the wonderful typography that they do. Of course it was impossible to connect the dots looking forward when I was in college. But it was very, very clear looking backwards 10 years later.

Again, you can't connect the dots looking forward; you can only connect them looking backwards. So you have to trust that the dots will somehow connect in your future. You have to trust in something – your gut, destiny, life, karma, whatever. This approach has never let me down, and it has made all the difference in my life.

My second story is about love and loss.

I was lucky – I found what I loved to do early in life. Woz [Steve Wozniak] and I started Apple in my parents' garage when I was 20. We worked hard, and in 10 years Apple had grown from just the two of us in a garage into a $2bn company with over 4,000 employees. We had just released our finest creation – the Macintosh – a year earlier, and I had just turned 30. And then I got fired. How can you get fired from a company you started? Well, as Apple grew we hired someone who I thought was very talented to run the company with me and for the first year or so things went well. But then our visions of the future began to diverge and eventually we had a falling-out. When we did, our board of directors sided with him. So at 30 I was out. And very publicly out. What had been the focus of my entire adult life was gone, and it was devastating.

I really didn't know what to do for a few months. I felt that I had let the previous generation of entrepreneurs down – that I had dropped the baton as it was being passed to me. I met with David Packard and Bob Noyce and tried to apologise for screwing up so badly. I was a very public failure, and I even thought about running away from the valley. But something slowly began to dawn on me – I still loved what I did. The turn of events at Apple had not changed that one bit. I had been rejected, but I was still in love. And so I decided to start over. I didn't see it then, but it turned out that getting fired from Apple was the best thing that could have ever happened to me. The heaviness of being successful was replaced by the lightness of being a beginner again, less sure about everything. It freed me to enter one of the most creative periods of my life.

During the next five years, I started a company named NeXT, another com-

pany named Pixar, and fell in love with an amazing woman who would be-come my wife. Pixar went on to create the world's first computer-animated feature film, Toy Story, and is now the most successful animation studio in the world. In a remarkable turn of events, Apple bought NeXT, I returned to Apple, and the technology we developed at NeXT is at the heart of Apple's current renaissance. And Laurene and I have a wonderful family together.

I'm pretty sure none of this would have happened if I hadn't been fired from Apple. It was awful-tasting medicine, but I guess the patient needed it. Some-times life hits you in the head with a brick. Don't lose faith. I'm convinced that the only thing that kept me going was that I loved what I did. You've got to find what you love. And that is as true for your work as it is for your lovers. Your work is going to fill a large part of your life, and the only way to be truly satisfied is to do what you believe is great work. And the only way to do great work is to love what you do. If you haven't found it yet, keep looking. Don't settle. As with all matters of the heart, you'll know when you find it. And, like any great relationship, it just gets better and better as the years roll on. So keep looking until you find it. Don't settle.

My third story is about death.

When I was 17, I read a quote that went something like: "If you live each day as if it was your last, some day you'll most certainly be right." It made an impression on me, and since then, for the past 33 years, I have looked in the mirror every morning and asked myself: "If today were the last day of my life, would I want to do what I am about to do today?" And whenever the answer has been "no" for too many days in a row, I know I need to change something.

Remembering that I'll be dead soon is the most important tool I've ever en-countered to help me make the big choices in life. Because almost everything – all external expectations, all pride, all fear of embarrassment or failure – these things just fall away in the face of death, leaving only what is truly important. Remembering that you are going to die is the best way I know to avoid the trap of thinking you have something to lose. You are already naked. There is no reason not to follow your heart.

About a year ago I was diagnosed with cancer. I had a scan at 7.30 in the morning and it clearly showed a tumour on my pancreas. I didn't even know what a pancreas was. The doctors told me this was almost certainly a type of cancer that is incurable and that I should expect to live no longer than three to six months. My doctor advised me to go home and get my affairs in order, which is doctor's code for "prepare to die". It means to try to tell your kids everything you thought you'd have the next 10 years to tell them in just a few months. It means to make sure everything is buttoned up so that it will be as easy as possible for your family. It means to say your goodbyes.

I lived with that diagnosis all day. Later that evening I had a biopsy, where they stuck an endoscope down my throat, through my stomach and into my intestines, put a needle into my pancreas and got a few cells from the tumour. I was sedated, but my wife, who was there, told me that when they viewed the cells under a microscope the doctors started crying because it turned out to be a very rare form of pancreatic cancer that is curable with surgery. I had the surgery and I'm fine now.

This was the closest I've been to facing death, and I hope it's the closest I get for a few more decades. Having lived through it, I can now say this to you with a bit more certainty than when death was a useful, but purely intellectual, concept:

No one wants to die. Even people who want to go to heaven don't want to die to get there. And yet death is the destination we all share. No one has ever escaped it. And that is as it should be, because death is very likely the single best invention of life. It is life's change agent. It clears out the old to make way for the new. Right now the new is you, but some day not too long from now, you will gradually become the old and be cleared away. Sorry to be so dramatic, but it is quite true.

Your time is limited, so don't waste it living someone else's life. Don't be trapped by dogma – which is living with the results of other people's thinking. Don't let the noise of others' opinions drown out your own inner voice. And, most important, have the courage to follow your heart and intuition. They somehow already know what you truly want to become. Everything else is secondary.

When I was young, there was an amazing publication called the Whole Earth Catalogue, which was one of the bibles of my generation. It was created by a fellow named Stewart Brand not far from here in Menlo Park, and he brought it to life with his poetic touch. This was in the late 1960s, before personal computers and desktop publishing, so it was all made with typewriters, scissors and Polaroid cameras. It was sort of like Google in pa-perback form, 35 years before Google came along: it was idealistic, and overflowing with neat tools and great notions.

Stewart and his team put out several issues of the Whole Earth Catalogue, and then, when it had run its course, they put out a final issue. It was the mid-1970s, and I was your age. On the back cover of their final issue was a photograph of an early morning country road, the kind you might find your-self hitchhiking on if you were so adventurous. Beneath it were the words "Stay hungry. Stay foolish". It was their farewell message as they signed off. Stay hungry. Stay foolish. And I have always wished that for myself. And now, as you graduate to begin anew, I wish that for you. Stay hungry. Stay foolish."

Steve Jobs died December 2011, aged 56.

Now some people never take the time out to take stock of where their life is going, so here's another exercise for you. I call it the 'Rocking Chair' exercise.

Again, find somewhere comfortable and sit back and relax as discussed ear-lier in the book. Close your eyes and focus on your breathing, noticing each in-breath and out-breath, and slowly let your breathing rate slow down.

Now, when you are suitably relaxed allow your mind to drift off into the future, way, way, off until you can imagine yourself as a wise old person, sitting in a rocking chair looking back along the time-line of your life, back to where you are now at this point in time.

At first I want you to view things from the perspective of the old 'you' in the rocking chair.

As that old person looking back at the 'you' that you are now, take a good look at the route your life has taken from where you currently are at this present moment in your life to where 'you' will be as that old person look-ing back. Look at the route that your life has taken if nothing was to change between now and then. Look at the things that will have occurred and the life that you will have led to get you from where you are now to where the old wise 'you' is sitting in the rocking chair.

Now I want you to switch perspectives. I want you to look from where you are now towards the old wise 'you' sat in the rocking chair looking back at you.

I want you to see the direction your life is taking you panning out in front of you towards the old 'you' sat in the rocking chair. I want you to study it and look at what is likely to occur and where your life is taking you if nothing was to change in your present circumstances.

Now here are some tough questions. Is that the life you wish to lead? Are those the things you wish to occur? And is that what you want to do en-route to becoming the 'you' who will end up sitting in that rocking chair looking back?

If the answer to any of those questions is no, then start making changes right now to change what you will experience or what is likely to occur so that you can live the rest of your life without any regrets.

The fact is this, once you reach the rocking chair and start looking back it will be too late to change the past. If you want to change your future you need to do it now while you still can, because you can't change your past.

What stops people making changes in their lives is fear of failure. But the only sure way to never fail is to never try. In addition, failure itself can also be a blessing in disguise.

CHAPTER 9
Failure – A Blessing in Disguise

Some time ago I heard Anthony Robbins give a lecture, and he said: *"How many people here like surprises?"* to which the vast majority of the audience responded by putting their hands up and said yes. *"Liars"*, Robbins replied; *"you only like the surprises you want, the ones you don't want you call problems"*.

What Robbins knew was that failure or hardship can often be a blessing in disguise if we look for the seed of equivalent benefit at every given opportunity.

Failure can open new doors of opportunity and provide us with useful knowledge of the realities of life through trial and error, and it also gives us an opportunity to notice what doesn't work which gives us more room for growth. In fact failure can lead to outcomes far greater than what could have been foreseen had the failure not occurred.

You have probably heard about the story of Thomas Edison who took over 10,000 attempts to create the light bulb. However you may not be aware that Edison's first failure came when his teacher sent him home from school with a note advising his parents that he could not take an education. This so shocked the young Edison that he acquired an education that enabled him to become a truly great inventor. Had he not have been sent home from school he may never have mustered the motivation to become such a brilliant and tenacious inventor.

Einstein, one of the greatest scientists of a generation, was also a competent failure. Like Edison, Einstein failed at school too. He clashed with authorities and resented the school's regime and teaching methods. He later wrote that the spirit of learning and creative thought were lost in strict rote learning. As a result Einstein never really had any formal schooling but, like Edison, continued with his own education, yet failure didn't stop there.

After eventually graduating Einstein searched unsuccessfully for a teaching post for many years and was almost resigned to failure until in the end a former classmate's father helped him secure a job in a patent office as an assistant examiner. Yet his failures didn't stop there either. Whilst working as a lowly assistant examiner he was continually passed over for promotion and therefore had no prospect of moving on or away from his daily mundane routine. Yet instead of simply resigning himself to failure Einstein decided to make the best use of his current position.

As an assistant examiner much of Einstein's work in the patents office related to questions about transmission of electric signals and electrical-mechanical synchronisation of time, and it was this work that eventually led Einstein to his radical conclusions about the nature of light and the fundamental connection between space and time.

In short, had Einstein not failed as an academic student, not failed in finding a teaching position and not failed in securing any promotional prospects, Einstein's theory of relativity, and much of the modern technology we have today as a result of his work, may never have existed.

Thank goodness for failure!

And these greats are not alone. There are many, many other failures that have led to great successes. The inventor of the post-it note was actually trying to invent a bonding agent that once applied would create a permanent fixing that could not be removed. His failure in achieving that lead to the discovery and development of the very post-it note that now probably sits on your desk.

The failures of Abraham Lincoln in retail, surveying, soldiering, and the practice of law, turned his talents in a direction which prepared him to become the greatest President, the United States of America has ever known.

Failure is a blessing or a curse, depending upon your reaction to it. However, the majority of people give up hope and quit at the first sign of failure, even before it overtakes them. Successful people however, in every walk of life, see failure as a means of feedback and as an accurate measuring device to allow them to fine-tune their progress towards their desired outcome.

Over the next two months I want you to attempt as many new things as you can. Start with simple things such as trying new foods, going to new places, etc. But when you do, take everything that you didn't quite like, not as failure but as feedback. This will allow you to make better choices next time you try something new and not restrict you from never trying again. By doing this, you may discover things about you that you didn't know and things that you will like that you will have never known about, had you not tried something new. Then simply apply this new strategy to you life. If you want to write a book start writing. Start by writing a small report or, if you are a good cook, start writing a book that contains a few recipes. If you wish to become a trainer start training, run a small course locally and build from there. If you wish to do charity work find a local charity. If you wish to become more spiritual go to a church, temple or mosque or find a local Buddhist temple if you wish to learn to meditate and then start running local meditation courses yourself. The opportunities are endless once you start, but I think that you are getting the picture.

Think about it, if you did one thing each day and simply analysed the feedback to improve what you did next time, can you just imagine how far you will have gone in only two months – remember the 50 folds of paper?

Now imagine this, if you did that consistently for one whole year, how far do you think you will have progressed? One thing is most definitely certain, you will be a million miles ahead of those who either have done nothing or who simply gave up at the first sign of failure.

Remember this: *"If you reach for the stars, one thing is for sure, you won't end up with a handful of mud."*

One thing that we can do to help this process is to keep things in perspective because sometimes a small problem can become a big one due to our ability to distort reality, and if we allow that to happen we can lose sight of the bigger picture. Therefore, I thought that I would provide you with a link to a video that may help you keep your eye on your goal:

http://youtu.be/58fs5yI8K9I

Tip 6: Do not fear failure because the only way you will never fail is if you never try.

CHAPTER 10
The Arrow of Time

"When your past takes up a lot of your time, you can lose out on the future you really want."

Imagine there is a bank that credits your account each morning with £86,400, but at the end of every day whatever part of the balance you fail to use during the day is deleted. What would you do with the money available to you? Well, if you were a sensible person you would draw out every pound and use it, of course.

Well each of us has such a bank, and it's a bank named 'TIME'. Every morning it credits you with 86,400 seconds. Invest the day's deposits well, or the loss is yours. Just remember this: you can always make money, but you can never buy time, and I think that because our time is so limited on this planet, we should at least spend a little time finding out exactly what time is all about and how we can use it to our best advantage.

So, what is time?

Time is simply the ordering of events into sequences, one step after another. For example, we are born, we get older and eventually we will die. This is a sequence of events that moves in that direction, and no matter how we may try to change it, that is the direction that time takes us in. That is the order and sequence of all life.

In his brilliant television series, Wonders of the Universe, Professor Brian Cox talks about the nature of time. He says that: *"Events always happen in the same order, they are never jumbled up, and they never go backwards"*. For example, a glacier will move slowly towards the sea and when it reaches its destination, chunks of the front of the glacier will break off and fall into the water below. That is the order and sequence of events, and you would never expect to see that sequence happen in reverse – water molecules turning into ice, jumping out of the sea and attaching back on to the front of the glacier. There is a scientific explanation for this, and it is called the 'Arrow of Time'.

In short, the 'Arrow of Time' states that we are compelled to travel into the future, and that is because the Arrow of Time dictates that as each moment passes, things change and once these changes happen they are never undone.

This means that permanent change is a fundamental part of what it means to be human. We all age as the years pass by. We are born, we live and then we ultimately die. This is the joy and tragedy of our lives. It is the circle of life. Everything in the universe changes with time, nothing remains constant. Everything is irreversibly changing.

So what does this mean to you and me? This means that none of us can change what has already happened; so living in the past is merely an exercise in memory. Constantly reliving unpleasant and traumatic past events only serves to imprison us in a state of mind that locks us into a moment in time that has already passed. And while you live in the past, time is still moving on because it doesn't stand still for anyone or anything. That means that if you choose to live in the past you choose to remain locked in a time zone that time has now left behind.

Tip 7: Let the past remain in the past and move forward. Take immediate action right now. Take massive immediate action. Don't wait until it's too late, as time will not stand still for you. Make the most of your time and you can do that right now by making a list of all of the things that you are going to do.

CHAPTER 11
The Second Law of Thermodynamics and Entropy

One of the most important laws in physics for understanding the evolution of the universe and the passage of time is the 'Second Law of Thermodynamics'.

The reason the 'Second Law of Thermodynamics' is so profound is because at its heart it contains a radically new concept – something physicists call 'entropy'.

Entropy explains why, when left to the mercy of the elements, seemingly permanent structures like buildings fall into disarray and collapse.

A good way to understand how and why this happens is to think of objects not of single things, but of being made up of many different parts, like individual grains of sand that would make up a pile of sand.

Entropy is basically a measure of how many ways we can re-arrange grains of sand while keeping the sand pile relatively the same, and, according to Professor Cox, there are literally trillions and trillions of ways that can be done. For example, imagine you were sat next to a pile of sand on a beach and you simply, randomly messed the sand up and moved the sand around with your hand and made another pile. Although the pile would be different it would in many ways still be similar to what you started with – a pile of sand. In the language of entropy the sand pile has 'high-entropy' because there are many ways in which its state or shape can be re-arranged with it still remaining a pile of sand.

However, if we decided to create some order by placing the sand from the disordered pile in a castle-shaped bucket, compressed it down and up-turned the bucked, just like you see children doing at the seaside, we could end up with a sand castle. Now lets assume that there are as many individual sand-grains in the sand castle as there were in the pile of sand prior to it being placed in the bucket. However, anything we now do to it will mess up the ordered structure of the sand castle, and because of that the sand castle is referred to as having 'low entropy' because the grains of sand are in a much more ordered state.

So, just to summarise, a pile of sand which has many ways of re-arranging the sand grains without changing the structure equals high entropy, very few ways of rearranging the sand grains in the sand castle without changing its structure, without disordering it equals low entropy.

Eventually, if left to the elements you can easily imagine what will happen to the sand castle. The winds will blow the sand around and take sand from the castle and deposit it somewhere else. In short the sand castle will disintegrate and basically fall to bits. What is happening is that the wind is taking sand off the sand castle and depositing it somewhere else and in doing so it is making a pile of sand elsewhere.

Now there is nothing in the laws of physics to say that the sand that is blown away could not deposit itself into another ordered structure – another sand castle for example, but that is very highly unlikely to occur, and the reason is because there are very few ways to organise the sand into a castle because it is a low entropy structure – the odds are simply stacked against it if you like. It is much more likely that when the wind blows the sand around it will simply deposit it into a pile of sand – a high entropy structure.

This is because entropy will always increase from low to high, and the reason is because it is simply overwhelmingly more likely that it will.

But what does all of this, mean to us?

Well, we all like an ordered life of structure and routine, which means that we are always striving to create a life of 'low entropy' design if you like. But no matter how hard we try to avoid it, things will happen in our lives that will upset that order and routine and move us from a low entropy lifestyle into a high entropy state where our lives, like grains of sand, can be blown in different directions. Why, because entropy always increases and time only runs in one direction.

We see this in our families when our children grow up. When they are young they are dependent on us and we create order and routine for them, but as they get older they change and this can cause great disharmony and upset for the child and their parents if this aspect of change isn't understood.

In his book 'Intimate Behaviour', Desmond Morris suggests that each child goes through three stages: *"Hold me tight"*, *"Put me down"* and *"Leave me alone"*.

This cycle first becomes apparent in a child's early years, when the child moves from the *"hold me tight"* phase (characteristic of infancy) to the *"put me down"* stage when the child first begins to crawl and walk and in doing so achieves some independence and autonomy from its parents.

In adolescence, *"leave me alone"* becomes the predominant phase as the child struggles to form its own individual identity and this can be a very challenging and difficult time for the child as well as its parents. However, most experts will tell you that this is a normal and necessary phase in a child's adolescent development.

The difficulty for the parent however, is that while their child is crying *"leave me alone"* the parent needs their *"hold me tight"* needs to be met as that is what they feel their child needs. In short, the parents 'low-entropy model' is being changed as their child moves from a 'low entropy' stage in its life to a 'high entropy' adolescent stage. But that is the natural order and sequence of how children develop.

Children going through adolescence are also dealing with very 'complex issues' and this is why adolescence can be a very challenging time for them and their parents. The light at the end of the tunnel however, is that one day all of this chaos will end because these stages are transient stages and, given the right love and support, the vast majority of children will 'emerge' from these transitory stages a more mature, wiser and well-rounded person. The best advice I can give you, as a parent is this – never give up on your child. Even if they give up on themselves, you must never give up on them. And don't lose hope or sight of the fact that what you are being exposed to and what your child is experiencing will one day end, and this will become clearer to you as you read the next chapter.

For now just understand this. The one consistent fact of life is that change will happen and the more we try and hold onto permanent fixtures in our lives the more we will experience suffering and disappointment. True happiness therefore, is in moving forward and not dwelling on the past and in accepting change as a fundamental fact of life.

Tip 8: Embrace change and look for the positive benefit in it. Do not hold onto the past, especially past hurts and traumas. Let them go. Your life is moving forwards so there is no point living in the past. And never give up.

CHAPTER 12
Impermanence

In Buddhism the concept of impermanence plays a central role in Buddhist thought and is a key practice. Contemplation of impermanence serves two main vital functions within Buddhism. On a conventional level, or in an everyday sense, the Buddhist practitioner contemplates his or her own impermanence – the fact that life is tenuous and we never know when we will die. When this reflection is combined with a belief in the rarity of human existence and the possibility of attaining a state of spiritual liberation, then this contemplation enables the practitioner to use his or her time to their best advantage.

On a deeper level, the contemplation of impermanence is designed to help the practitioner understand the true nature of reality, and through this understanding, dispel the ignorance that is the ultimate source of their suffering.

Now this is important to Buddhists, but does the contemplation of impermanence have any practical application in the everyday lives of non-Buddhists as well?

Well if we view the concept of *"impermanence"* from the perspective of *"change"*, then the answer is a definite yes, because no matter how you look at it the fact remains, life is all about change and if we refuse to accept this fact and resist the natural changes that life will bring, then we will continue to perpetuate our own suffering and live a delusional existence.

For example, if you are fifty or sixty years young there is no point wishing you were twenty-one again. If you were married or had a partner for thirty years and you are now separated or maybe going through a less than pleasant divorce, then there is no point in wondering what could have been had you not have spent that time together. What matters most is what you do from now on. Holding on to the past is creating permanent suffering from something that no longer exists. Time has moved on.

The acceptance of change therefore, can be the one most important factor in reducing most of our self-created suffering. For example, if we define our own self-image by what we used to look like and what we used to be able to do that we cannot do now, it is a safe bet that we will not get any happier as we get older, if we carry these regrets with us into our future.

In essence therefore, the Buddhist concept of impermanence is a practical concept that we can all apply in our daily lives. It can help us move forward by accepting that nothing lasts forever and by contemplating on our own mortality and the mortality of our family and close friends, it can help us put things into context by helping us to realise that change happens on every scale, from within our own individual lives to that of our families, our work and ultimately the universe within which we all live.

Most importantly, impermanence helps people to focus on the present moment and on what is happening right here and right now. By focussing on what is happening right here and right now, you can find true happiness by actually living in the moment.

This is a great gift, especially as so many of us are caught up in the mind-set of what may happen in the future or what has happened in the past, whether we have the newest iPhone, the biggest house, or the newest car, etc. And many people strive all of their lives to have these material objects at the expense of spending quality time with those that they love. Then disaster strikes and someone close to you dies or becomes ill, or you become ill, and then the focus of what is important changes dramatically because change has been imposed on you.

When this happens many people will feel guilty and some even cheated because the very things that they have been working and striving to provide, at the expense of the time spent doing so, no longer becomes important. In such circumstances many people will begin to realise that they may have wasted valuable and precious time that they can no longer get back. What becomes important to them now is making the most of the little time left with those that they love. Accepting impermanence therefore grounds people in reality, by helping them to be grateful for what they have right here and right now. How many material possessions would you trade in, to have good health and peace of mind?

By accepting impermanence and change in our lives we can turn our minds towards what we have now instead of always looking to the past or worrying about the future. Impermanence also means that we can accept that in time everything will change because nothing lasts forever, and that includes any misfortune, hurt, pain and distress that you have ever encountered in your life or that you maybe encountering right now. As time moves on the permanence of the pain, distress and hurt will lessen because time is also one of Mother Nature's great healers.

Tip 9: Be grateful for what you have now. Think how lucky you are just to be able to get out of bed each morning. Life is for living and life means change. So, you can start by changing your attitude, by focussing on what you can be grateful for and enjoying each moment that you are alive.

CHAPTER 13
Finding meaning in our suffering

During periods of crisis and suffering it can seem almost impossible for many of us to find any positive meaning in what is happening. The common response in most people is "Why me?" yet the ability to find meaning and a purpose in our suffering is possibly one of the greatest survival aids that we possess, and to illustrate this fact to you I would like to share the story of a man called Victor Frankl, whom I also wrote about in my book Understanding Quantum Thinking'.

Victor Frankl, a Jewish psychiatrist imprisoned by the Nazis in the Second World War, once said: *"Man is ready and willing to shoulder any suffering as soon and as long as he can see meaning in it."*

During the Second World War, Viktor Frankl used his brutal and inhumane treatment in the concentration camps as a way of finding meaning to his existence. A religious man, Frankl accepted that there must be a purpose in his being there so he used his time at the camps to gain an insight into how some people survived the camps and why others perished.

His conclusion was that survival wasn't based on youth or physical strength but rather on the strength derived from finding one's purpose in any given situation and the meaning attributed to it.

Now finding meaning in suffering, is without doubt a powerful method of helping us cope, but it is not an easy task, and for Frankl it must have been a very difficult task indeed, because during the time he was in the camps, his father, mother, brother and wife died in the bestial and brutal conditions they were forced to live in or were gassed to death. With the exception of his sister, his entire family died or were executed in the Nazi concentration camps.

In addition to this, Frankl at times had to live with up to fifteen hundred other captives in a shed that was built to hold no more than two hundred and where there was not enough room to lie down or squat on the bare, cold ground. For those that could, they would be sharing that space with the urine and excrement of other malnourished prisoners due to the lack of proper toilet and hygiene facilities. And as for food, a five-ounce piece of bread was at times the only food they might have to eat in a four-day period.

As a result of the endless drudgery, bitterness, cold, hunger, the primitive and inhumane conditions, the constant danger of death and the sense of hopelessness of their situation, the thought of suicide was always present in the minds of many. Yet one fact was clearly evident to Frankl and that was that it was a person's attitude towards the situation they found themselves in, not the situation itself that determined how they coped and ultimately whether they survived or not. What Frankl found was that those who survived the situations they found themselves in, had to adopt certain ways of thinking and behaving.

Frankl soon realized that it was not what happened to him that was important. He had no control over any aspect of his environment and he was aware of the fact that the Nazi's could do whatever they wanted with his emaciated body. They could not, however, control his inner identity, nor could they control how he could choose to respond in any given set of circumstances. He decided therefore, to control his inner self. He saw that there was a gap between what happened to him and his reaction, and in that gap he had the power and freedom to choose his response. He even knew that he could be randomly pulled out and shot by the Nazi's for no other reason apart from the fact that he was Jewish, and that he could do nothing about that fact. That was the extreme extent of the lack of control he had in the environment he was in. However, what he chose to do was decide that if that day came, he would choose how he would face death. Even with the ever-present threat of death looming over him like the 'Sword of Damocles', Frankl found a way to find something he could maintain control over.

In short, Frankl refused to accept that his situation was hopeless. He maintained his ability to make decisions and choices. He didn't resign himself to the apathy of 'learned helplessness'. Frankl became aware of the fact that his own choices, not his circumstances, defined his identity. No matter how bare or brutal his environment, he was in control of how he would choose to respond. If he could do that in the brutal and inhumane conditions that he found himself in for year after year, then so can each and every one of us – if we choose to do so.

To be able to do this in times of crisis however, it would be best to practice this ability when things are going well. As we all know, a tree with the strongest roots can withstand the most violent of storms, but such roots do not magically appear when a storm appears on the horizon.

This is why practice is important. Practice an attitude of gratitude every moment you can. Be grateful for your life and the simple fact that you are alive, have enough food to eat, are in possibly good health, etc., and don't get caught in the trap of finding reasons to moan or complain about things that are really not that important like; what shall we watch on TV tonight, what to eat for tea, which restaurant shall we go to, and when there, what shall we pick from the menu of seemingly limitless options? These are not issues worth worrying about, and if you need some motivation watch this:

http://youtu.be/j97frMQGJL8

What will you do today?

Tip 10: Take control of your life and never give up hope. Find a purpose in your life to give meaning to what you do. As Steve Jobs said: *"If today were the last day of my life, would I want to do what I am about to do today? And whenever the answer has been "no" for too many days in a row, I know I need to change something"*. Change is the key to your happiness; so don't squander the opportunity by resisting it. Embrace it and go with the flow.

CHAPTER 14
Mindfulness Meditation

One of the ways in which you can train your mind, which can also have a seriously positive effect on your life, can be found in the practice of meditation.

Research is now showing that meditation can have a major positive impact on our health and wellbeing. For example, in a study reported in the MIT News 5th May 2011, MIT and Harvard neuroscientists explain why the practice helps tune out distractions and relieve pain. The study, published online in April 2011 in the journal Brain Research Bulletin, found that people trained to meditate over an eight-week period were better able to control a specific type of brain waves called alpha rhythms.

"These activity patterns are thought to minimise distractions, to diminish the likelihood stimuli will grab your attention," says Christopher Moore, an MIT neuroscientist and senior author of the paper. *"Our data indicate that meditation training makes you better at focusing, in part by allowing you to better regulate how things that arise will impact you."*

The subjects trained in meditation also reported that they felt less stress than the non-meditators. *"Their objective condition might not have changed, but they're not as reactive to their situation,"* Kerr says. *"They're more able to handle stress."*

In another report published in The Times newspaper on 14th March 2008 Kathy Sykes, who holds the chair in the Public Engagement of Science and Engineering at Bristol, stated that she has long known that if she does not find at least 30 minutes a day in her frantically overcrowded schedule to lie down and listen to music, she is grumpier, more tired and less able to concentrate.

What Professor Sykes did not realise until recently is that she was, in effect, practising a fairly crude form of meditation. She also didn't know that there was growing evidence to show that this ancient practice can make people healthier and happier. It may even increase life span; alter brain structure and change personality.

Ancient traditional therapies do not always stand up to close scientific scrutiny, but when Professor Sykes put meditation under the metaphorical microscope for the second BBC series of Alternative Therapies: The Evidence, she was surprised to find that the saffron-robed monks of Kathmandu and the white-coated scientists of Harvard shared more common ground than might have been expected.

There are now signs that mainstream medicine has already started to sit up and take notice of meditation. Mindfulness-based cognitive therapy (MBCT), which is about 80 per cent meditation, has been approved by the National Institute for Health and Clinical Excellence (NICE) for use with people who have experienced three or more episodes of depression.

In yet another report, initially published on 1st May 2001 and last reviewed on the 3rd September 2010, it has also been shown that as little as 10 minutes of meditation a day can help squash anxiety,

Many other studies have also shown that meditation not only has a mental but also a profound physiological effect on the body and these studies have shown that, among other benefits, meditation can help reverse heart disease, reduce pain and enhance the body's immune system, enabling it to better fight disease.

More new research offers even more additional encouragement. In a study published in the journal Stroke, 60 African-Americans with atherosclerosis, or hardening of the arteries, practiced meditation for six to nine months. (African-Americans are twice as likely to die from cardiovascular disease as whites). The meditators showed a marked decrease in the thickness of their artery walls, while the non-meditators actually showed an increase. The change for the meditation group could potentially bring about an 11 per cent decrease in the risk of heart attack and an 8 - 15 per cent decrease in the risk of stroke.

A second study, published in Psychosomatic Medicine, taught a randomised group of ninety cancer patients mindful meditation (another type of practice). After seven weeks, those who had meditated reported that they were significantly less depressed, anxious, angry and confused than the control group, which hadn't practiced meditation. The meditators also had more energy and fewer heart and gastrointestinal problems than the other group.

Other recent research has looked at precisely what happens during meditation that allows it to cause these positive physical changes. Researchers at the Maharishi School of Management in Fairfield, Iowa, found that meditation has a pervasive effect on stress. They looked at a group of people who had meditated for four months and found that they produced less of the stress hormone cortisol. They were therefore better able to adapt to stress in their lives, no matter what their circumstances were.

Now you may have tried meditation and found it difficult, but actually meditation is relatively easy to do. All it involves is focussing on something, normally your breath or paying full attention to what you are doing at any given moment in time and if you have been practicing the breathing and visualisation exercise at the beginning of this book then you have been practicing mediation.

One of the great Meditation Masters is a Buddhist Monk called Thich Nhat Hanh (who was nominated for the Nobel Peace Prize by the late Dr. Martin Luther King), and his book 'The Miracle of Mindfulness' is a great way to understand the concept and practice of mindfulness meditation. The beauty of what Thich Nhat Hanh explores is how mindfulness can be applied to everyday tasks like; washing the dishes and going for a walk. It is a great book for beginners and even for the more experienced meditator.

Another good book is 'Mindfulness – a practical guide to finding peace in a frantic world' by Mark Williams and Danny Penman. This book is very good because it is based on scientific research into mindfulness meditation at Oxford University and provides meditation exercises that are easy for non-Buddhists to use. It also comes with an accompanying cd with all of the meditation exercises on it. I have personally used it and have found it to be a very good resource.

CHAPTER 15
A Summary of Tips

Tip 1: Be definite in your positive outlook to life. Set your sights on what you want as opposed to what you don't want, and you can start by changing all negative thoughts to positive ones. Engage all of your senses in doing this, just as you did when you were a child.

Tip 2: Consciously and continually make every effort to only program information and data via the tools of autosuggestion and self-talk that is both positive and beneficial.

Tip 3: Make a conscious decision to simply not read or watch anything that will leave a negative impression in your mind, like muddy footprints on your carpet. Just as you would ask someone to remove their dirty or muddy shoes before entering your home, instruct yourself to restrict entry to the 'home' of your intellect by leaving anything that can 'muddy' your thoughts outside of the entry to the house of your mind.

Tip 4: Replace negative criticism with positive self-talk at every opportunity.

Tip 5: Consciously make the effort to find the benefit in everything you do. Decide to now ignore any negativity or doubt. Yet should negativity occur consciously rise above it and direct your mind back to finding the positive seed of equivalent benefit in any given situation.

Tip 6: Do not fear failure because the only way you will never fail is if you never try.

Tip 7: Let the past remain in the past and move forward. Take immediate action right now. Take massive immediate action. Don't wait until it's too late, as time will not stand still for you. Make the most of your time and you can do that right now by making a list of all of the things that you are going to do.

Tip 8: Embrace change and look for the positive benefit in it. Do not hold onto the past, especially past hurts and traumas. Let them go. You life is moving forwards so there is no point in living in the past. And never give up.

Tip 9: Be grateful for what you have now. Think how lucky you are just to be able to get out of bed each morning. Life is for living and life means change. So, you can start by changing your attitude by focussing on what you can be grateful for and enjoying each moment that you are alive.

Tip 10: Take control of your life and never give up hope. Find a purpose in your life to give meaning to what you do. As Steve Jobs said: *"If today were the last day of my life, would I want to do what I am about to do today?"* And whenever the answer has been *"no"* for too many days in a row, I know I need to change something. Change is the key to your happiness; so don't squander the opportunity by resisting it. Embrace it and go with the flow.

CHAPTER 16
Endnote

My wish for you is that this book will inspire and motivate you to take control over you life by taking control over the way you choose to think. By doing this you can decide to choose what to think about and what meaning and purpose you can derive from everything that happens to you, from this point onwards. As Mahatma Ghandi said *"Be the change you want to see in the world"*.

The development of your mind is in your hands and your destination in life will be set by the choices you make and the information you choose to put into your mind.

That fertile field of unending possibility, your unconscious mind, has the capacity to produce any crop from the seeds you choose to plant, so always sow positives and look for a seed of equivalent benefit in everything you do. If Victor Frankl can survive the horrors of the Nazi concentration camps by finding his purpose and a meaning in his life, you too can surely find meaning and purpose in yours.

Also, remember that the arrow of time only moves in one direction and it doesn't stand still or wait for stragglers. We actually have to choose to live in our past because the moment time moves forward all that is left is a memory of a time since gone. Therefore, I urge you to move with the times and accept change as part of life.

Live a good life but don't be too hard on yourself. Don't set too many rigid rules as everything turns back into 'piles of sand' eventually so don't expect anything to be a permanent fixture in your life. That way you can never be disappointed. Everything is impermanent. Accept and understand that and you will most certainly overcome suffering.

Finally, do not lose sight of where life is leading you. We are all heading towards a common goal which is death, and no matter how we try to ignore it or put it to the back of our minds, death is a common destination that we all share. Therefore do not fear it nor fight it. Death is simply a part of life and proof that nothing lasts forever. Therefore, become grateful for what you have whilst you are alive, and don't waste precious time living someone else's dream. Find your own. Find something you love doing and do more of it.

Do something every day that moves you forward either personally, intellectually, spiritually, or even financially. And remember, if you did that every day for fifty days how much positive change you will have achieved.

And as you are achieving think about what good you can do with it. Think about who you can help along the way. Life is about living and one of the greatest gifts we have is the capacity for compassion and love. Therefore maximise your ability to be compassionate and loving and you will most definitely be the richest person on earth.

About the Author

Mark Dawes is a successful businessman, a much sought-after consultant and possibly one of the most inspirational and motivational speakers and trainers in the UK today. He is also the author of 'Understanding Quantum Thinking', a fascinating insight into how our minds work.

As well as being a National Sports Coach, a Cognitive Hypnotherapist and Master Practitioner of NLP (Neuro-Linguistic Programming), he has studied and researched many other fields of personal and professional interest including Positive Psychology, Cognitive Behavioural Therapy, Neuro-Associative Learning, Stress and Combat Psychology and Quantum Mechanics.

Mark has had a varied and interesting career including service in the Royal Navy and as a Hostage Negotiator. He has also worked as an Expert Witness with his evidence used in a report by The House of Lords and House of Commons Joint Committee on Human Rights. He has also appeared on Sky and BBC news as well as various local and national radio programmes.

Connect with Mark

Mark's Website: http://www.markdawes.com or http://www.nfps.info

Mark's Blog: https://markdawes.wordpress.com

Facebook: http://www.facebook.com/mark.nfps

Twitter: https://twitter.com/#!/markdawescom

NOTES